FIRST PEOPLES

THE NAVAJO

OF NORTH AMERICA

GERALD M. KNOWLES

Lerner Publications Company • Minneapolis

**First American edition published in 2003
by Lerner Publications Company**

Published by arrangement with Times Editions
Copyright © 2003 by Times Media Private Limited

Lerner Publications Company
A division of Lerner Publishing Group
241 First Avenue North
Minneapolis, MN 55401 U.S.A.
Website address: www.lernerbooks.com

Series originated and designed by
Times Editions
An imprint of Times Media Private Limited
A member of the Times Publishing Group
1 New Industrial Road, Singapore 536196
Website address: www.timesone.com.sg/te

Series editors: Margaret J. Goldstein, Oh Hwee Yen
Series designers: Tuck Loong, Rosie Francis
Series picture researcher: Susan Jane Manuel

Library of Congress Cataloging-in-Publication Data
Knowles, Gerald M.
The Navajo of North America / by Gerald M. Knowles.
p. cm. — (First peoples)
Summary: Introduces the history, modern and traditional cultural
practices, and modern and traditional economies of the Navajo people of
the southwestern United States, as well as information about the
landscape, fauna, and flora of the region.
Includes bibliographical references and index.
ISBN 0-8225-0662-9 (lib. bdg. : alk. paper)
1. Navajo Indians—History—Juvenile literature. 2. Navajo
Indians—Social life and customs—Juvenile literature. 3. Navajo
Indians—Ethnobiology—Juvenile literature. [1. Navajo Indians. 2.
Indians of North America—Southwest, New.] I. Title. II. Series.
E99.N3 K574 2003
979.1004'972--dc21   2002001870

Printed in Malaysia
Bound in the United States of America

1 2 3 4 5 6—0S—08 07 06 05 04 03

CONTENTS

WHO ARE THE NAVAJO?

The Navajo are one of the largest Native American groups in the United States. They number approximately 200,000. They live in the Navajo Nation, located in the southwestern part of the United States. The Navajo Nation lies within the borders of three states—Arizona, New Mexico, and Utah. It covers 16 million acres (6.5 million hectares) of land. It is the biggest Native American reservation in the country.

Their Own Name

The Navajo language is also called Navajo. The language belongs to the Athabascan family, a group of languages common to many Native American groups in Canada and North America. The Navajo call themselves and their language Diné, which means "the people."

Navajo Neighbors

The Navajo live together with other Native American groups such as the Hopi and the Zuni. The Navajo share land with the Hopi in northeastern Arizona. The Zuni live just south of the Navajo Reservation. The Navajo have learned many skills from their neighbors. The Hopi, for example, taught the Navajo how to farm. Starting in the 1500s, the Navajo and their neighbors fought many wars with foreigners, including the Spanish. Unlike neighboring groups, however, the Navajo were never conquered by the Spanish.

COLORADO

ROCKY MOUNTAINS

Mount Hesperus
(13,232 ft / 4,033 m)

UTAH

Colorado River

San Juan River

Navajo Mountain
(10,388 ft / 3,166 m) Monument Valley

Grand Canyon

Tuba City

Black Mesa

Tsaile

Canyon de Chelly

Chaco Canyon

Hopi Indian Reservation

Chinle

Navajo Nation

Gallup

San Francisco Mountain
(12,633 ft / 3,851 m)

Mount Taylor
(8,000 ft / 2,438 m)

ARIZONA

NEW MEXICO

N

FOUR SACRED MOUNTAINS

To the north of the Navajo Nation lies Mount Hesperus; to the south, Mount Taylor; to the east, Blanca Peak; and to the west, San Francisco Mountain (*left*). The Navajo people consider these mountains sacred. According to Navajo myth, the creator placed the Navajo in the area bordered by the four mountains. The mountains represent the four points of the compass: north, south, east, and west.

THE NAVAJO LANDSCAPE

The landscape of the Navajo Nation includes deserts, canyons, mountains, grasslands, and plateaus. Many valleys cut through the land. Ridges and small hills also dot the landscape. Standing almost 9,800 feet (2,987 meters) above sea level, the Chuska Mountains are the highest points of the Navajo Nation.

Below: Buttes—isolated blocks of rock—tower above the terrain of Monument Valley in Utah. The Spanish named the three buttes on the far right of this picture the Three Sisters. They thought the buttes resembled three nuns wearing habits.

Changing Weather

The weather in the Navajo Nation changes from season to season. High temperatures range from 90 to 110 degrees Fahrenheit (32.2 to 37.8 degrees Celsius) in summer. Winter temperatures often fall below the freezing point. The deserts receive about 6 inches (15.2 centimeters) of rain per year, and the mountains receive about 12 inches (30.5 centimeters).

Riches Beneath the Earth

Many areas on the Colorado Plateau, such as Black Mesa and Coal Mine Canyon in Arizona, are rich in coal. In fact, the Navajo Nation contains one of the world's largest stores of coal. Natural gas and oil lie in the basin of the San Juan River in northeastern Navajo Nation. The land is also a source of precious minerals such as turquoise and silver.

High above Sea Level

Much of the Navajo Nation sits atop a highland region known as the Colorado Plateau. Most of the plateau is made of shale, a layered rock that's rich in clay. Black Mesa, an elevated stretch of land in Arizona, is one of the most spectacular features of the area. It stands at about 8,000 feet (2,438 meters) above sea level. It has a width of 75 miles (120.7 kilometers) and a length of 100 miles (160.9 kilometers).

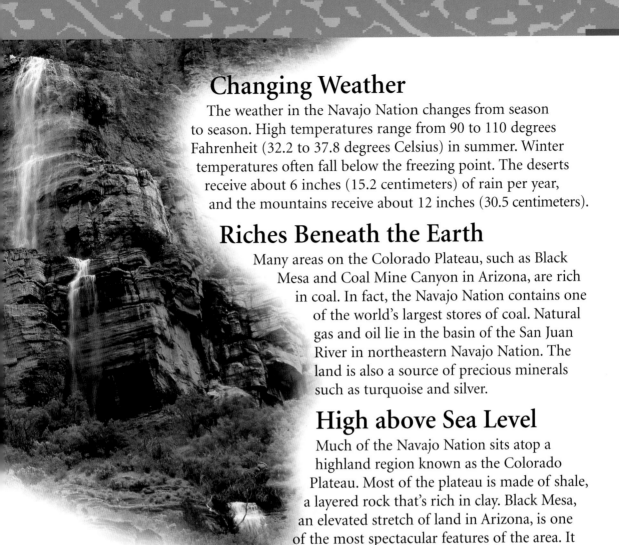

Above: The Cheyava Falls of Arizona

THE PAINTED DESERT

The Painted Desert stretches along the southwestern edge of the Navajo Nation. This desert is named for the streaks of white quartz, amethyst (a purple quartz), and yellow crystals that color the landscape in beautiful shades. Some of these rocks are approximately 200 million years old. At about 4,900 feet (1,494 meters) above sea level, the Painted Desert is the lowest point of the Navajo Nation.

PLANTS ON THE LAND

A wide variety of plants grows in the Navajo Nation. Pine and spruce trees thrive on the highest slopes. Forests of cedar, juniper, and oak cover mid-level slopes. At lower elevations, willow and cottonwood trees line the banks of streams.

Native Plants and Trees

Native plants in the Navajo Nation include yucca and piñon. The yucca plant has long, stiff leaves and a woody stem. Its flowers are white. Piñon trees have dome-shaped canopies that can reach 30 feet (9 meters) in height. These trees produce edible nuts. Sagebrush, juniper trees, and prickly pear cacti are also native to the Navajo Nation. Many parts of the Navajo Nation receive very little rainfall. The plants cope with the dry environment in various ways. Prickly pear cacti, for example, store water in their hollow stems. Sagebrush roots grow deep beneath the ground to reach water.

Left: Yucca plants are common on the mesas and desert plains of the Navajo Nation. These plants can reach 13 feet (4 meters) in height. The Navajo use the yucca plant in many ways. They make shampoo by soaking the leaves and roots of the plants in water. This mixture is also a good salve for sunburns and scratches.

Left: Piñon nuts are a favorite food in the Navajo Nation. The piñon tree is a relative of the pine tree.

Food Crops

The Navajo plant crops such as melons and corn in the valleys of the Navajo Nation. Rivers supply water for the crops throughout the year. Since the late 1600s, the Navajo have also planted fruit trees. The Hopi taught them to grow peach trees. Navajo farms are small, usually less than 2 acres (0.8 hectares) in size.

Useful Plants

Every autumn, the Navajo harvest piñon nuts for food. Piñon pitch, the dark, thick sap of the tree, is a good treatment for cuts and sores. Sagebrush is another useful plant. The Navajo boil its leaves and stems to make tea, which is a good treatment for the flu. Many plants produce dyes. The Navajo boil the leaves and twigs of the juniper tree to make orange and yellow dye. The juice of the prickly pear makes beautiful rose-colored dye.

MAGICAL CORN

The Navajo respect all plants. Corn (*right*) is one of the most sacred plants in the Navajo Nation. The Navajo believe that corn is the food of the gods and that offerings of cornmeal bring success in life. Corn pollen is said to weaken evil forces. The pollen represents happiness, prosperity, and peace. When the Navajo pray for corn pollen to cover the paths of loved ones, they are praying for blessings for their loved ones.

ANIMALS OF THE NAVAJO NATION

Before the Spanish came to the Southwest, the Navajo did not own any animals except turkeys and dogs. The Spanish brought goats, cows, horses, and sheep to the land of the Navajo. Of these animals, sheep and horses were the most useful. Sheep provided meat for food and wool for clothing. Horses became the main form of transportation in the land of the Navajo.

On the Plains

The grasslands of the Navajo Nation are home to antelope, deer, and bighorn sheep. But their numbers have dropped in recent years. In fact, fewer than sixty bighorn sheep are left in the Navajo Nation. Hunters have killed some of the animals. In addition, grazing lands have been taken over by sheep and cattle ranches.

Left: Wild animals such as this black-tailed deer cannot thrive without large amounts of grassland for grazing.

Up in the Mountains

Mountain lions, black bears, and bobcats roam the mountains and plateaus of the Navajo Nation. Black bears have beautiful smooth, black fur and weigh between 135 to 350 pounds (61.2 to 158.8 kilograms). Of all animals, the Navajo fear and respect the black bear most. They believe that black bears harbor evil spirits. When someone kills a black bear, its evil spirit enters the person's stomach and causes great discomfort.

Up in the Sky

Many colorful birds make their homes in the Navajo Nation. These birds include the river-dwelling marsh wren, a small brown bird with streaks down its back, and the tree swallow, a beautiful blue bird with a white throat. These birds are less than 6 inches (15.2 centimeters) long. Bigger birds such as bald eagles soar above the land. Bald eagles have wings spanning up to 8 feet (2.4 meters) long.

Above: The Navajo consider eagle feathers sacred objects. The Navajo sometimes wear eagle feathers in their hair as a sign of respect for their dead relatives.

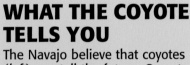

WHAT THE COYOTE TELLS YOU

The Navajo believe that coyotes (*left*) can tell the future. One story tells of a Navajo boy who grew up with coyotes. One day, the boy's coyote mother told him he was a human and let him return to his people. Because he could understand the language of coyotes, he could interpret what they said about the future. The Navajo boy left home every morning to listen to the coyotes. Upon his return, he told his family what was going to happen.

THE NAVAJO APPEAR

Archaeologists believe that the ancestors of the Navajo migrated from Asia to Alaska more than fifteen thousand years ago, using a land bridge to cross the ocean. The bridge has since been covered by water. The ancestors of the Navajo lived in present-day Alaska and Canada for thousands of years. Then they traveled south, arriving in the American Southwest by about A.D. 1000.

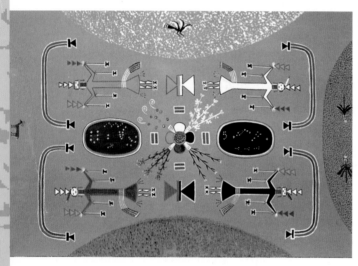

Creation Stories

The Navajo have a different story about their origins. They believe that they emerged from Gobernador Knob, a mountain in northern New Mexico. According to their myths, the Supreme Being created fire, air, water, and pollen. The pollen became earth. Then the Supreme Being made the Holy People, the creators of humankind. The Holy People also made the natural world and its animals and plants.

Above: This sand painting shows the Navajo Holy People. They helped create the first humans.

The Four Worlds

According to their myths, the Navajo passed through three underground worlds to reach this world. The first world, the Black World, was full of insects. First Man lived in the first world. Together with the insects, he moved up to the second world—the Blue World. There, animals such as the mountain lion and the coyote were created. First Woman appeared in the next world, the Yellow World. First Man and First Woman started to argue. This displeased the Supreme Being. He sent a flood to the Yellow World. First Man and First Woman survived by climbing up a reed out of the third world to the fourth world, called the Glittering World, on the earth's surface.

Above: By the 1600s, the Navajo had settled in the grasslands northwest of Santa Fe, New Mexico.

Hunter Gatherers

The early Navajo were nomads, people who do not have permanent homes. They traveled from place to place, using spears to hunt game such as prairie dogs, rabbits, and birds. They gathered piñon nuts and the fruit of prickly pear cacti. Influenced by the Hopi, the Navajo started to plant food crops such as corn, beans, and squash. The Navajo had to stay near their farms to sow, weed, and harvest the crops. They could not travel as much as they did before. But they did not give up their hunting and gathering lifestyle altogether.

A CHANGING CLIMATE

Scientists think that up to about six thousand years ago, the American Southwest had a wetter climate than it does in modern times. Many arid regions of the present-day Navajo Nation were covered with freshwater lakes. Scientists think that the multicolored minerals of the Painted Desert came from places as distant as the Rocky Mountains. Floods of water carried the minerals south to Arizona.

WAR WITH THE SPANISH

In 1540 the Spanish arrived in the Navajo Nation. They established settlements along rivers in Texas and New Mexico. Farmers, herders, silversmiths, and other craftspeople were among the Spanish settlers. They set up towns and farms and began to raise sheep and other animals. By observing the Spanish, the Navajo and other Native American groups learned to eat sheep's meat and use sheep's wool for weaving.

Below: Canyon del Muerto, where, in 1805, the Spanish killed 115 Navajo in a battle for land

Above: A Navajo military leader

Navajo Raiders

When the Navajo saw how useful horses, goats, and sheep were to the Spanish, they started raiding Spanish settlements and stealing livestock. The raids angered the Spanish. They attacked Navajo bands entering their farms and grazing areas. But because the Navajo were seminomadic, the Spanish found it difficult to locate and attack Navajo settlements. As a result, the Navajo escaped Spanish control.

Massacre at Canyon del Muerto

In 1805, 5,000 Navajo invaded the Spanish town of Seboyeta, near Mount Taylor in New Mexico. The Navajo were trying to reclaim land around Mount Taylor, one of their sacred mountains. The Spanish army fought back. The bows and arrows of the Navajo were no match for the rifles, lances, and swords of the Spanish soldiers. When the Navajo realized they were losing the battle, they left Seboyeta. The Spanish pursued them. At Canyon del Muerto, the Navajo hid in a cave. But the Spanish discovered them and fired into the cave, killing 115 Navajo. The Navajo call this place Massacre Cave.

Learning from the Spanish

As a group, the Navajo were never under Spanish rule. However, the Spanish sometimes captured Navajo children and made them slaves. The children had to prepare meals for the Spanish, herd their sheep and cattle, and groom their horses. As a result, these Navajo became skilled at caring for livestock.

PUEBLOS BECOME ALLIES

Although the Navajo kept their independence, the Spanish conquered many of their neighbors, including the Pueblo Indians of the Rio Grande valley. The Pueblo were skilled weavers and farmers. The Spanish conquerors took away the Pueblo's farms and enslaved them. In 1680 the Pueblo revolted against the Spanish and went to live among the Navajo. The Pueblo taught the Navajo the art of weaving.

THE UNITED STATES TAKES CONTROL

In 1846 the United States waged war on Mexico. The fighting lasted two years. In 1847 the U.S. Army captured Mexico City. One year later, Mexico surrendered a vast stretch of territory to the United States, encompassing much of the American Southwest. The Navajo and other Native American groups in the Southwest then came under U.S. rule.

The Long Walk

Angered by Navajo attacks on white ranches, the U.S. government declared war on the Navajo in 1863. General Kit Carson led U.S. troops through Navajo lands, burning homes and crops and slaughtering livestock along the way. The soldiers captured and enslaved Navajo women and children. Without their crops and livestock, the Navajo faced the threat of starvation. In the winter of 1864, eight thousand Navajo marched into Fort Defiance, Arizona, and surrendered to the U.S. Army. The army sent the Navajo to prison camps at Fort Sumner in eastern New Mexico. The Navajo had to make the 300-mile (482.8-kilometer) journey on foot. Many Navajo died on the trip.

Left: Kit Carson and his horse, Apache

The Coyote Tells the Future

The Navajo performed many ceremonies, asking their gods to return them to their homeland. In one such ceremony, a headman by the name of Barboncito caught a female coyote. He made the coyote face east. A circle of Navajo surrounded the coyote. Barboncito put a shell in the coyote's mouth and then released it. The coyote turned clockwise and walked toward the west. This was a sign to the Navajo that they would return west to their homeland. Indeed, in 1868, the U.S. government allowed the Navajo to return to their homeland.

Above: Navajo shamans performing a ceremony

MORE ROOM TO LIVE

The Navajo Reservation originally measured 3.5 million acres (1.4 million hectares) across the border of New Mexico and Arizona. In 1878 the U.S. government expanded the reservation westward. More than fifteen expansion projects followed. The Navajo named the land Navajo Nation in 1969. The nation is run by the Navajo Nation Council, elected by the Navajo people. The seal (*left*) of the Navajo Nation shows 50 arrowheads, representing the 50 U.S. states.

TWENTIETH-CENTURY CHANGES

When the United States was formed in the late 1700s, Native Americans were not considered citizens of the new nation. They were forced onto reservation land. They were denied many rights, including the right to vote.

Gradually, Native Americans gained equal rights. In 1924 the U.S. government granted citizenship to all Native Americans born in the United States. By the mid-1900s, most states had granted the Navajo the right to vote.

The Stock Reduction Program

In the early 1930s, the U.S. government discovered that the grazing areas in the Navajo Nation had lost much of their grass. To protect the grasslands, the U.S. government began the Stock Reduction Program. The government ordered the killing of 50 percent of all Navajo sheep, horses, and cattle feeding on pasture. The Stock Reduction Program resulted in less meat to feed the Navajo people and fewer farms to provide jobs. Many of the Navajo fell into poverty. The Navajo started to leave their homes and farms to look for jobs in the cities.

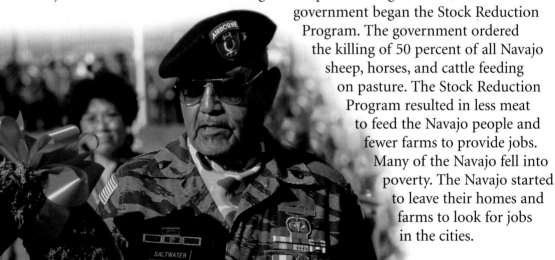

Left: A Navajo war veteran

The Nation Goes to War

Above: This photograph, taken in 1943, shows the 297th U.S. Marine Platoon at San Diego. What is so special about this platoon? Every single one of its members is Navajo.

When the United States entered World War II in 1941, more than 3,600 Navajo volunteered their services to the U.S. military. Navajo men fought on the battlefields, while many Navajo women worked for the Red Cross. The military sent Navajo soldiers to fight in Europe and the Pacific. Some Navajo men worked as "code talkers." They helped the marines create secret codes using the Navajo language. World War II ended in 1945. Many Navajo soldiers could not find jobs when they returned home.

The War on Poverty

By the mid-1900s, many Navajo were so poor they could not feed their families. Fifty percent of Navajo children died of starvation before they reached five years of age. During the 1960s, the U.S. government started a program called the War on Poverty. Part of the program involved creating the Office of Navajo Economic Opportunity. This department provided jobs for the Navajo and taught them about their native culture. It also tried to improve the health and education level of Navajo people. Many Navajo worked for this agency.

NAVAJO COMMUNITY COLLEGE

In 1968 the Navajo Nation Council established the Navajo Community College (*left*). The name was later changed to Diné College. Located in Tsaile, Arizona, the school was the first Navajo-run college in the United States. It teaches typical academic courses, as well as classes in Navajo history, culture, language, and philosophy .

THE OLD ECONOMY

The early Navajo practiced subsistence agriculture. They grew only what they needed to feed themselves. After the Spanish arrived, the Navajo began to raise sheep, which provided a ready source of meat in their diets. As their farms grew larger, the Navajo sometimes had small surpluses of food. They exchanged the extra food for vegetables from neighboring Hopi villages. They also traded woven products for food.

Division of Labor

In early Navajo society, the men were in charge of hunting wild game and gathering plants. Women took care of the sheep and farms. Women did most of the weaving, although they sometimes taught men in their families how to weave. After the Navajo were moved to the reservation, men could no longer hunt in the forests beyond the reservation. They started helping the women herd and farm.

Traditional Crafts

Traditionally, the Navajo wove their own clothing. They made tunics, belts, shirts, and blankets both to wear and to trade. The Navajo traded with nomadic Native American groups, who took Navajo products to distant places. By the 1700s, people living as far away as Montana owned Navajo blankets. The Navajo made silver and turquoise jewelry. They learned the art of silversmithing from Spanish craftsmen.

Above: A Navajo couple fashion jewelry. Many Navajo learned silversmithing after World War II.

Below: Sheepherding on a farm in the Navajo Reservation, Monument Valley

SPECIAL SHEEP

Herding sheep (*below*) is a traditional activity that the Navajo still practice. Among Navajo sheepherders, the Navajo-Churro sheep is a popular breed. These sheep are descendants of sheep brought by the Spanish in the 1500s. They can weigh up to 175 pounds (79.4 kilograms) and might have apricot, white, gray, black, beige, or brown fleece. Navajo-Churro sheep are relatively easy to look after. They are highly resistant to many diseases. Twice a year, sheepherders shear the animals using hand clippers. The fleece of Navajo-Churro sheep is low in lanolin, a fatty substance. This kind of fleece absorbs dyes easily.

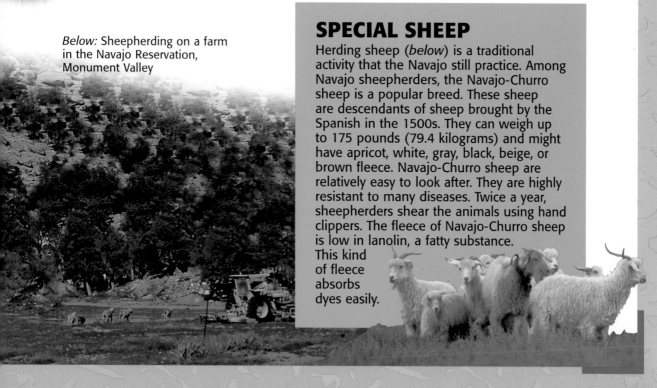

NEW WAYS TO MAKE A LIVING

After the Stock Reduction Program, many Navajo herders started to seek jobs outside the Navajo Reservation. They moved to the cities to work for factories or railroads. Most of those who left the reservation were men. Women stayed behind to look after the sheep, farms, and families. Some Navajo who stayed on the reservation took up new kinds of work, in industries including tourism and government service.

Wealth from Mining

In the 1920s, energy companies discovered coal, oil, and gas on Navajo lands. The companies wanted to mine these valuable resources. They signed leases, agreeing to pay the Navajo for the right to use the land and mine the resources. Since mining began, the Navajo Nation has received more than $1.8 billion from mining leases. For the past fifty years, coal mining has provided the major source of income for the Navajo Nation.

Left: Navajo crafts for sale at a Navajo trading post. During the days of captivity at Fort Sumner, the U.S. Army fed the Navajo rations of coffee, sugar, and flour. The Navajo learned to like these foods, which they had never had before. When the Navajo returned to their homeland, white traders set up trading posts there. The traders supplied the new foods and other products in exchange for Navajo wool, rugs, and jewelry.

Above: A tourist admires a Navajo rug.

The Tourist Trade

Many Navajo work in the tourism industry as waiters, maids, and guides to the Navajo Nation's numerous tourist attractions, including Monument Valley and the Painted Desert. Tourists also visit Navajo communities and trading posts. Hubbell Trading Post in Ganado, Arizona, is a national historic site that is popular with tourists. It is the oldest operating trading post in the Navajo Nation.

Public Service

Many Navajo work for the Bureau of Indian Affairs. The bureau is a federal agency committed to guarding the welfare of all Native American peoples. The bureau runs many agencies in and around the Navajo Nation, with offices in Crownpoint and Shiprock, New Mexico, and Chinle, Tuba City, and Fort Defiance, Arizona. These agencies help build schools and roads and provide health services in the Navajo Nation.

FAMOUS NAVAJO JEWELRY

An American businessman named Fred Harvey brought Navajo silver jewelry to the world. Arriving in the Southwest in the late 1800s, Harvey admired the jewelry he saw at trading posts in the Navajo Nation. He saw a business opportunity. His company supplied Navajo craftspeople with the raw materials they needed to produce jewelry. The company then sold the jewelry in tourist shops. By the 1930s, people all over the world knew about Navajo silver jewelry.

TRADITIONAL HOGANS

The Navajo traditionally lived in homes made of juniper branches, bark, and earth. The homes were called hogans. According to some Navajo myths, the coyote built the first hogan. In other stories, the gods made the first hogan.

In earlier eras, homes had no electricity or running water. The Navajo gathered water from wells. They stored it in pitchers made from piñon wood. They used candles, lamps, and torches to light the inside of their homes. They use firewood for cooking.

Below: A Navajo family in front of a male hogan, the first kind of Navajo house. By the 1900s, male hogans were no longer used for housing. Male hogans were instead used for religious ceremonies and to store grain or hay.

The Forked-Stick Hogan

The forked-stick hogan, also known as the male or cone-shaped hogan, was the first dwelling of the Navajo in the Southwest. To build it, the Navajo leaned four forked poles against one another and filled the spaces between the poles with earth. They left a small hole in the ceiling to serve as a smoke hole, or chimney, and a larger space for a door. The forked-stick hogan was used up through the 1700s. At that time, the Navajo were still mainly a hunting and gathering society.

Above: A male hogan

The forked-stick hogan was a good home for people who moved often. It was easy to assemble and took less than a day to build. But it was also small and cramped.

The Family Home

Female hogans began to appear in the early 1800s, as the Navajo became more settled. Female hogans were six- or eight-sided homes. They were much larger than male hogans—up to 10 feet (3 meters) high and 23 feet (7 meters) wide. The Navajo originally built female hogans by piling juniper logs on top of one another. The logs interlocked at the corners. In the 1900s, as more railroads began to cross the Southwest, the Navajo started using wooden railroad ties as building materials.

SHADE IN THE SUMMER HEAT

During summer, Navajo families lived in summer hogans located near their crop fields. These summer hogans were usually square, with a pole at each corner. Some summer hogans were round (*right*). Rows of thin poles served as walls. The poles had gaps between them, allowing summer breezes to enter the hogan and keep it cool. The Navajo made a roof from juniper boughs and leaves.

THE NAVAJO SHEEP CAMP

Navajo sheepherding communities are called sheep camps. In the past, there were four female hogans and one male hogan in each camp. One family lived in each female hogan. Everyone in the camp was related. In the 1960s, modern houses began to appear in Navajo sheep camps.

House Rules

Female hogans had only one room. Men and women slept in different parts of the room. They slept on animal furs and mats woven from yucca plants. Family members had to observe various rules inside the hogan. Men always sat in the southern portion of the room, and women sat in the northern portion. Visitors sat in the western portion. This part of the room faced the door and was the place of honor. When the Navajo entered their hogans, they moved in a clockwise direction, from east to south to west to north. This practice was based on the Navajo belief that the sun moved in a likewise fashion.

Below: Modern-style houses and buildings at a modern-day farm in the Navajo Reservation

Above: A female hogan behind a sweat house. The sweat house is an important part of many Navajo dwellings. In the sweat house, the Navajo pour water over heated rocks to make steam. The Navajo sit in the steam and sweat. They believe sweating helps to purify their spirits.

Modern-Style Homes

In the late 1900s, modern houses began to replace hogans in major Navajo towns, such as Kayenta, Arizona. Many of the dwellings were two-stories high, with running water, electricity, and telephones. Organizations such as the Utah Navajo Development Council and the U.S. Department of Housing and Urban Development provided the money to build the houses. The houses were built at low cost, so even Navajo without a lot of money could afford to buy them.

LIVING AND BREATHING HOMES

The entrances of hogans always face east. The Navajo believe that as the sun rises in the east, its blessings enter the hogan through the door. The Navajo also believe that the four poles of the male hogan represent the four sacred mountains. To the Navajo, hogans are living things. They breathe through the smoke hole, through which families' prayers rise to the gods in heaven.

LIVING WITH THE NAVAJO

The basic unit of Navajo society is the family, which includes the children and their parents. Families are usually quite big, with up to six children in each. Extended family members, such as aunts, uncles, and cousins, help one another with farmwork.

Below: Women are the heads of Navajo families. They are in charge of weaving and herding. Women also make important religious and political decisions in the sheep camp. In the late 1900s, Navajo women led the effort to reintroduce Navajo-Churro sheep into their farms.

Eating Navajo Style

Mothers pass traditional Navajo recipes to their daughters by word of mouth. Kneel-down corn is a traditional Navajo dish. It is made from mashed corn stuffed into cornhusks and roasted under burning coals.

Above: Women in Navajo families cook most of the meals.

Corncakes are another favorite dish. They are made of ground corn patties, pan-fried in oil. Fry bread is probably one of the most famous Navajo dishes. It is made from flour, salt, and water, formed into thin pieces of dough and fried. Navajo families eat fry bread at dinner with stew or corn-on-the-cob.

Left: Fry bread. Good fry bread is crispy and slightly salty.

Tending the Flocks

Navajo sheepherders start the day with a visit to the grocery store, where they stock up on foods to eat while herding. Then they gather their herds from a pen and take them to the pasture to graze. Sheep that walk slower than the rest of the flock wear bells. The clanging of the bells helps sheepherders keep track of the slowest animals. Sometimes the sheepherders carry stones in tin containers. When they rattle the containers, the noise urges the herd along.

COUNTING SHEEP

Up to the 1970s, Navajo herds contained as many as four hundred sheep. But herds have gotten smaller and smaller. Some modern-day herds have fewer than twenty sheep. The decline has occurred as more Navajo have taken jobs in the city. They no longer want to be sheepherders. Retiring herders often sell their sheep to outsiders when they cannot find younger Navajo to take over their herds.

GROWING UP NAVAJO

Navajo children are taught myths and stories early in their lives. The Navajo believe that stories help children think, and thinking is an important process to the Navajo. They believe that the Holy People spent a long time thinking about creation before they made the world. They also believe that the right thoughts can produce harmony in life and can prevent or cure illness. The right thoughts encourage respect for sacred things. They are not focused on greed, ambition, or worry.

Below: A Navajo grandmother feeds her grandchild. Navajo parents teach children about their ancestors and relatives. Children learn to respect their elders and how to treat both relatives and non-relatives.

Above: The Navajo master the art of horseback riding at an early age. Many Navajo children grow up to compete in rodeos.

Early Lessons

When Navajo children are between four and six years old, their parents start to tell them Navajo legends. The legends teach children about the natural forces that shaped the world: earth, fire, water, and air. The legends also teach children that they must respect these forces. Children also learn to honor the hogan, which protects the Navajo family.

Jobs for Children

Starting around age seven, Navajo children must help their parents herd, take care of livestock, and build fires for warmth and cooking. Like the men in the Navajo community, boys learn to gather firewood. Like their mothers, girls learn to cook, weave, clean, and throw away cooled ashes. Children between the ages of seven and nine receive three lambs from their parents. At this age, they learn to pray at dawn and at sunset.

The Adult World

About age thirteen, children become adults. After age twenty-two, they begin to think about having a family and helping the community. At age thirty, the Navajo begin to plan for the future. They learn to be responsible leaders and elders in the community.

IT'S UP TO YOU

Navajo parents give their children (*right*) a lot of freedom, even as infants. For example, children can go to sleep as late as they want. They do not have to eat three meals a day. They can eat whenever they feel hungry.

DRESSING FOR THE OCCASION

Many Navajo wear modern-style clothing, just like typical Americans. However, the Navajo wear traditional outfits when they attend social events or important ceremonies. The Navajo believe that the spirits will not recognize and bless them if they do not wear traditional Navajo dress.

Outfits for Men

In traditional dress, Navajo men wear long-sleeved velvet shirts, which are not tucked into their pants. Some shirts have ribbons hanging from the seams. Men in traditional wear also put on jewelry such as bracelets and necklaces. Some men wear their hair long and tie it into buns using yarn.

Right: A Navajo boy in Plains Indian costume dances at a powwow. The Navajo maintain close ties with other Indian groups. This boy shows his friendship with the Plains Indians by wearing their costume.

Traditional Women's Wear

When dressing traditionally, Navajo women wear long-sleeved blouses and pleated cotton or velvet skirts. Their hemlines often fall below the knee. Spanish families handed these items down to their Navajo servants and their families in the late 1800s.

Women sometimes tie sashes around their waists or wear belts decorated with turquoise. They also wear turquoise and silver jewelry. Navajo women wrap shawls around their shoulders.

Unmarried Navajo women usually leave their hair untied, but married women often tie it into buns, kept in place with white yarn.

Navajo Footwear

The Navajo wear moccasins on special occasions. The moccasins are made of deerskin and cowhide, with thick leather soles. Many moccasins are high boots, reaching all the way up to the knees. Navajo women often wear high moccasins that touch the bottom of their skirts. In this way, in keeping with Navajo tradition, the women do not reveal any of their skin below the waist. Everyday footwear includes cowboy boots and other modern-style footwear.

Above: Two Navajo women in traditional wear enjoy ice cream.

WEARING BLANKETS

The Navajo wear blankets as they would shawls, draped over the head or over one or both shoulders. The Navajo also wear blankets like vests, made by sewing two blankets back-to-back, with gaps to serve as the neckline and armholes. Before 1860 the majority of the Navajo wore blankets. In the late 1800s, Navajo women began to wear velvet blouses and gathered skirts like those worn by the Spanish.

THE TRADITIONAL ARTS

The Navajo learned the art of silversmithing from Spanish craftsmen and the art of weaving from the Pueblo people. The Navajo have modified these arts to reflect their own unique culture.

Navajo Weaving

Navajo weavers spin wool into yarn by hand, using a tool called a spindle. The yarn is then dyed. The most common colors are brown, green, red, and blue. Many Navajo weavings have stripes. Others have diagonal lines and steplike patterns. The Navajo do not learn their weaving designs from books. They learn directly from their mothers and grandmothers.

Right: A Navajo rug weaver spins wool into yarn.

Beautiful Silver Jewelry

The Navajo make all kinds of jewelry, including belt buckles, rings, bracelets, and necklaces. One design, commonly used on belt buckles, contains a row of stones set around a center gem.

Right: Navajo jewelers use many metals, including copper, brass, and iron, but silver is the most common metal.

The Sky Loom

The Navajo weave on a machine called a sky loom. It is a simple, upright wooden frame. Weavers first wrap strands up and down around the frame. Then, using a special fork, they insert strands sideways between the upright threads.

Left: The Navajo weave only during the day, because they believe that their textiles deserve to rest at night.

CHIEF BLANKETS

Navajo blankets and rugs are famous worldwide. The chief blanket is one of the most famous and one of the rarest Navajo woven items. Many chief blankets have stripes, diamonds, and crosses, in colors such as blue, white, black, and brown. The Navajo used to give chief blankets only to leaders of other Native American peoples. However, by the late 1800s, anyone could own a chief blanket. The blankets were very valuable. To get one, a person had to trade twenty horses, one hundred buffalo hides, or fifty dollars in gold. In modern-day markets, Navajo chief blankets can cost tens of thousands of dollars.

NEW ART FROM OLD ART

The Navajo still produce traditional arts and crafts. But they have also modified their traditions in modern times. For instance, in earlier eras, Navajo wove mainly to clothe themselves. But modern Navajo weavers produce works of fine art that people all over the world display in their homes and offices. Navajo musicians have also adapted to modern times. They sometimes use traditional instruments to make beautiful contemporary music. They also play traditional music with modern instruments.

Navajo Artists

The people and landscape of the Navajo Nation have inspired many Navajo painters. They include R. C. Gorman of New Mexico and Shonto Begay of Arizona. Gorman paints pictures of traditional Navajo woman. Begay paints scenes from everyday Navajo life. Both artists enjoy international fame.

Left: Navajo musicians at a powwow

Navajo Figurines

The Navajo started creating figurines, or small statues of animals and people, in the 1870s. Early artists molded the figurines out of mud. By the 1960s, artists were carving the pieces out of cottonwood. Modern figurines often combine traditional and contemporary images. A typical modern piece might show a Navajo in traditional dress riding in a Volkswagen.

Lots of Music

Traditionally, the Navajo sang chants to accompany religious ceremonies and social events. The men usually led the singing. They sang in high-pitched, nasal voices. Musicians played drums, flutes, and other musical instruments. They played long, flowing melodies without strong beats. Musicians made many of their instruments by hand, using sunflower stalks, cedar wood, and the hides of deer and cows. Modern-day Navajo musicians use both traditional and contemporary Navajo instruments.

Above: Some Navajo artists create figurines to show everyday Navajo life. This artwork shows a Navajo weaving on the sky loom, with her child snug and safe in a cradleboard next to her.

Right: The Navajo use the grandmother rattle, a traditional musical instrument, in their religious ceremonies to ward off evil.

CARLOS NAKAI

Carlos Nakai is one of many modern musicians who combine traditional Navajo music with modern influences. Nakai draws inspiration from his Navajo roots. He creates poetry with modern musical sounds, sprinkled with the cries of animals such as coyotes and eagles. Nakai uses many instruments in his work, including the synthesizer and wooden flutes.

THE NAVAJO LANGUAGE

Navajo is a very difficult language to speak. It has a number of sounds not heard in most languages. Of the 200,000 Navajo in the United States, approximately 70,000 no longer speak their native tongue. They generally speak only English. Other Navajo speak both English and Navajo.

Below: A Navajo parade at Gallup, New Mexico. The marchers carry a banner promoting Native American education. Political leaders and educators are working together on programs that teach the Navajo language in schools.

Navajo	English
Ah-KHAY-hay	Thank you
Bih-TOH	Spring
Dah-BEE	Sheep
DOH-ta	No
Hah-GO-nay	Goodbye
Hos-TEEN	Man
OH-wa	Yes
Shah-DON-nay	Friend
Shush	Bear
TOH	Water
Yaht-AY	Hello

The Sound of Navajo

A Navajo speaker uses the roof of the mouth and back of the throat to create sounds. Speakers raise or lower the pitch of their voices to change the meaning of words. Originally, the Navajo did not have a written language. They passed down tales and stories orally—by word of mouth. In the early 1900s, people wrote down Navajo words using the Roman alphabet.

Saving the Language

Many Navajo children no longer learn Navajo at home. The language could die out if children do not learn to speak, read, and write it. In 1984, the Navajo Nation made a rule stating that schools in the Navajo Reservation must teach the Navajo language. Modern Navajo students learn to speak, read, and write Navajo, in addition to studying English and other subjects. In some schools, such as Rock Point Community School in Arizona, students learn to read and write Navajo before they learn English.

THE NAVAJO CODE TALKERS

During World War II, the U.S. Marines sent coded messages. The Japanese, enemies of the United States, were able to break many of the codes. They could figure out what the marines were planning to do. So Navajo code talkers were asked to design a new code. The code talkers chose 500 English code words, which they translated into Navajo. The Navajo word for "egg" meant "bomb." The Navajo word for "our mother" meant the "United States." The Japanese could not break the Navajo codes. Thanks in part to the code talkers, the United States and its allies won the war.

HARMONY AMONG ALL THINGS

The Navajo believe that all things in nature are interconnected—that plants, animals, land, and people are all relatives, each with its own spirit. This harmony among things is called *hozho*. The Navajo believe that evil and sickness occur when hozho is broken. They hold religious ceremonies to attain hozho. Some ceremonies prevent illness. Others cure illness.

Right: The inside of a male hogan, where medicine people perform religious ceremonies. The ceremonies can last up to nine days.

Two Kinds of Healers

A Navajo who suffers from bad luck, poor health, or unhappiness will consult a hand trembler, or diagnostician. The diagnostician will enter into a trance. His or her trembling hands will move over the patient's body. The hands will stop trembling at the part of the body that is causing the illness. The diagnostician will then prescribe a ritual to heal the illness. Singers are also healers. They chant and make sand paintings (drawings in sand) on the hogan floor, sometimes with the help of a group of people. Once the sand painting is complete, the sick person sits on it. The singer blesses the patient with corn pollen and places sand from the painting on parts of the patient's body. The sand absorbs the evil that has caused the illness. When the ceremony is over, the singer destroys the sand painting.

Blessingway Ceremonies

Blessingway ceremonies prevent the breaking of hozho. Medicine people perform these ceremonies when the Navajo enter a new phase of life, such as puberty or marriage. The Navajo also use these ceremonies to bless buildings such as schools and hospitals. The blessings help keep harmony within the buildings. During a blessingway ceremony, the singer walks in a clockwise fashion inside a male hogan, spreading cornmeal on the ground and chanting prayers.

Right: A sand painter lets the material trail from his hand, forming a design on the ground.

PAINTING WITH SAND

Sand paintings are made with bits of colored rock, dyed sand, and powdery material such as charcoal and pollen. The biggest paintings can be 20 feet (6.1 meters) across. Sand paintings often feature animals such as eagles and snakes and plants such as corn. The paintings also show Navajo gods and spirits. The Navajo believe that when gods and spirits see themselves in the paintings, they enter the paintings. Thus, sand paintings are doorways that bridge the human and spirit worlds.

REST AND RELAXATION

The Navajo play both traditional and modern games. Many young Navajo enjoy basketball. Nearly every sheep camp has a backboard, and many young people take part in state basketball championships. The Navajo also enjoy cross-country races and other sports. Families and friends meet regularly at fairs, beauty pageants, and other social events. Rodeos are very popular. Many Navajo are skilled at horseback riding, cattle roping, and other rodeo contests.

The Shoe Game

The shoe game is one of the many traditional games that the Navajo play. This game is played for fun and at religious ceremonies. During this game, adults hide a ball under an overturned shoe. The shoe is lined up with five others. Children have to guess where the ball is. Children sometimes play the shoe game with their teachers in school.

Left: The Navajo spend a lot of time at rodeos. Every year, major rodeo events draw tourists to places such as Springerville, Arizona, and Bluff, Utah. The Navajo combine these rodeos with Navajo beauty pageants and powwows.

Powwow Weekends

Powwows take place every weekend in the Navajo Nation. Originally, Native Americans held powwows to ask the gods to protect warriors before battle. In modern times, powwows allow Native American people of different nations to meet together and relax. During powwows, the sound of music fills the air. Drummers sit and sing around a large drum that has a diameter of approximately 3 feet (91.4 centimeters). People also compete in events such as the jingle dance. During this contest, women from various Native American groups dance in traditional costumes, covered by 365 bell-like ornaments. Each of these ornaments represents a day of the year.

Right: Navajo at a powwow. The Navajo believe that powwows help Native Americans maintain unity.

SHARING DAY AND NIGHT

The Navajo enjoy listening to their own folktales. Some of these stories explain the natural phenomena the Navajo see around them. According to one Navajo story, animals of the daytime, such as the bear (*left*), and animals of the nighttime, including the coyote and the owl, once played the shoe game at night. The animals agreed that the winners of the game could decide to keep daylight or darkness forever. However, as dawn broke, the score was tied. Therefore, daytime and nighttime share the hours in a day.

SPECIAL CELEBRATIONS

The Navajo celebrate important life events. They hold special ceremonies to mark childbirth, marriages, and death. They also celebrate when a child becomes an adult.

Kinaalda—From Girl to Woman

At around age thirteen, Navajo girls perform the *kinaalda*, a four-day puberty ceremony. Afterward, the girl is considered an adult. She first washes her hair with soap made from the yucca plant. She then spends three days grinding more than 100 pounds (45.4 kilograms) of corn and wheat. She makes dough for a giant cornmeal cake. She digs a hole in the ground and lines it with corn husks. She bakes the cake in the hole, under burning coals, overnight. Throughout the night, the girl sits and watches the cake bake. Come dawn, she runs toward the sun and blesses the baked cake. She cuts it and offers the first piece to the sun and then serves the rest to her family and neighbors.

Releasing the Spirit

The Navajo believe that when a person dies, the good part of him or her leaves the body, but the evil part remains. Caskets are left unsealed to allow the dead person's spirit to escape from the earth. People are buried with items they cherished when they were alive, along with a set of clothes, a blanket, food, and water. The Navajo make sure there are no footprints around a grave. They believe that the footprints confuse the spirit guide who brings the dead away.

Above: An abandoned male hogan

Leaving the Hogan

The Navajo believe that evil spirits haunt the hogans of dead people after they die. Family members move out of the hogan to avoid the spirits. The Navajo have been following this practice since they were living in male hogans. In modern times, the Navajo often bring sick relatives to die in hospitals so that families do not have to leave home after a death.

THE SQUAW DANCE

In earlier eras, women performed the squaw dance (*left*) to welcome returning warriors. Modern-day Navajo perform this dance to protect sheep and to bless marriages and childbirth. The Navajo believe that the squaw dance brings good spirits to the Navajo Nation. Navajo men and women gather around a fire. The women dance around the fire and invite men to dance with them. The women receive gifts from the men after the dance.

GLOSSARY

archaeologist: a scientist who studies the remains of past human life and culture

arid: extremely dry

Athabascan family: a group of languages common to many Native American peoples in Canada and North America

buttes: isolated blocks of rock on a flat terrain. Buttes are usually formed by weathering and erosion.

headman: a leader or chief

hogan: a traditional Navajo home made of branches, bark, and earth

hozho (ho-ZOH)**:** harmony among things

hunter gatherers: people who hunt game and gather wild plants for food

kinaalda (kee-NAHL-dah)**:** a puberty rite a girl must experience before she is considered an adult in the community

land bridge: a narrow strip of land across a body of water

lease: an agreement allowing someone to use someone else's property for a certain period of time

mesa: a flat-topped piece of land with steep sides. Mesas are common in dry regions.

nomads: people who move from place to place, without a settled home

pitch: the dark sap of a tree

plateau: a large stretch of elevated land

reservation: a piece of government-owned land set aside for use by Native Americans

salve: a soothing ointment applied to burns, scratches, and cuts

sand painting: a drawing made of sand on the ground or the floor of a hogan

seminomadic: living a settled life sometimes, while traveling from place to place at other times

shamans: witch doctors who are able to communicate with the spirits

subsistence agriculture: growing just enough food needed for survival, without any surplus

FINDING OUT MORE

Books

Cohlene, Terri. *Turquoise Boy: A Navajo Legend*. Mahwah, NJ: Troll Associates, 1991.

Hunter, Sara Hoagland. *The Unbreakable Code*. Flagstaff, AZ: Northland Publishing, 1996.

Oughton, Jerrie. *The Magic Weaver of Rugs: The Tale of the Navajo*. Boston: Houghton Mifflin Company, 1994.

Roessel, Monty. *Kinaalda: A Navajo Girl Grows Up*. Minneapolis: Lerner Publications Company, 1993.

Roessel, Monty. *Songs from the Loom: A Navajo Girl Learns to Weave*. Minneapolis: Lerner Publications Company, 1995.

Sneve, Virginia Driving Hawk. *The Navajo: A First Americans Book*. New York: Holiday House, 1995.

Videos

Dineh Nation: The Navajo Story. Filmmakers Library Inc., 1991.

Seasons of a Navajo. Peace River Films, 1985.

Websites

<http://rcgormangallery.com>

<http://www.history.navy.mil/faqs/faq61-2.htm>

<http://www.navajo.org>

<http://www.navajo-churrosheep.com>

<http://www.navajoland.com>

Organizations

Navajo Nation Zoological and Botanical Park
P.O. Box 9000
Window Rock, AZ 86515
Tel: (520) 871-6573

Navajo Tribal Museum
P.O. Box 9000
Window Rock, AZ 86515
Tel: (520) 871-6673
Website: < http://www.navajoland.com/tourguide/attractions.html>

INDEX

ABOUT THE AUTHOR

Gerald M. Knowles holds a doctorate from the University of Illinois and a master's degree in education from the University of Northern Arizona. Gerald has worked intimately with the Navajo community on projects such as the Navajo Teacher Education Program (1973) and the Kayenta Township Project (1986). He is married and has five children.